YOUR JOURNEY TO FINANCIAL SECURITY

Investing
Credit
Planning
Budgeting
Financial Analysis

MICAH HOLLAND

"It's not how much money you make, but how much money you keep, how hard it works for you, and how many generations you keep it for."

Robert Kiyosaki

Your Journey to Financial Security

Step - By - Step Workbook

Micah Holland

Effective Financial Principles

Your Journey to Financial Security
"Step-by-Step" Workbook
Micah Holland

Published by Kingdom Publishing, LLC
1350 Blair Drive, Ste. H, Odenton, Maryland, USA

First printed in the United Sttes of America

Copyright (c) 2019

ISBN: 978-1-947741-46-1

This workbook is designed to provide accurate information regarding Finances.

"Your Journey to Financial Security" workbook and Micah R Holland are trademarks of MK Financial Services.

TABLE OF CONTENT

Your Journey to Financial Security

TABLE OF CONTENT (Cont.)

About
Micah R. Holland

After years of living beyond his means, Micah Holland took a hard look at his finances in the summer of 2003. What he discovered was a person in thousands of dollars of credit card debt and no plan. From that point forward, the journey began for Micah to figure out how to become financially stable. He created a basic budget, which showed his income vs. expenses for the month. To his dismay, Micah was in the red each month and like many Americans was "robbing Peter to pay Paul." After a few years of making some adjustments in his spending habits, along with a few increases in his salary, Micah began to see a light at the end of the tunnel. He began reading articles and taking financial courses in debt & credit management. In 2006, while at a seminar taught by a Home Mortgage Specialist affiliated with the local bank, Micah discovered his passion to help people with their finances. At that point in his life, Micah already was a homeowner, but was looking to create passive income by buying and selling homes for a profit. During the class, he heard several individuals frustrated because they were tired of hearing people say, "Just fix your credit" or "save 'x' amount of dollars," and you can buy a home. The main issue for people was that they didn't know how to accomplish the goal of saving money or fixing their credit.

Shortly after the seminar, Micah began putting information together on budgeting, goal setting and credit management. About 3 months later, he hosted his first seminar with a group of 10 individuals at his best friend's barbershop. The feedback regarding the material was overwhelmingly positive and had a tremendous impact on their finances.

Since 2006, Micah has conducted numerous financial seminars, workshops, and one-on-one sessions with individuals teaching the principles of personal finance.

Micah has an MBA in Business and is currently a resident of York, PA along with his wife and two kids.

Welcome

About 30% of Americans say they have more debt in credit cards and loans than money in a savings account for things like an emergency.

The bottom line is that Americans spend way too much and don't save enough.

Good news! If you are one of those Americans described above, you don't have to continue in that financial rut. The following information regarding budgeting, planning, credit evaluation, repair and investing can equip you with tools to become financially stable. It's important that you make an earnest commitment to use this knowledge and dedicate yourself to implementing a plan that will work for you and your family.

Owner's Pledge

Name: _____

Name: _____

Address: _____

_____

Date you started your financial journey: _____

What is your #1 reason for starting your financial journey?

_____

_____

_____

_____

_____

Understanding Money Management

Finance is a field that deals with the study of investments. This includes the dynamics of assets and liabilities over time under conditions of different degrees of uncertainty and risk. Finance can also be defined as the science of money management.

Personal finance revolves around protecting yourself against unforeseen personal events, paying for education, financing durable goods such as real estate and cars, buying insurance (e.g. health and property insurance), investing and saving for retirement as well as transference of family wealth across generations.

In today's culture, "get it now, pay for it later," it's very easy to not take debt seriously. It's damaging to accumulate a large amount of debt, and even more damaging not repaying it.

To avoid the pitfalls of debt and start your journey to accumulating wealth, this workbook is going to focus on a 5-step process that will help individuals become better money managers.

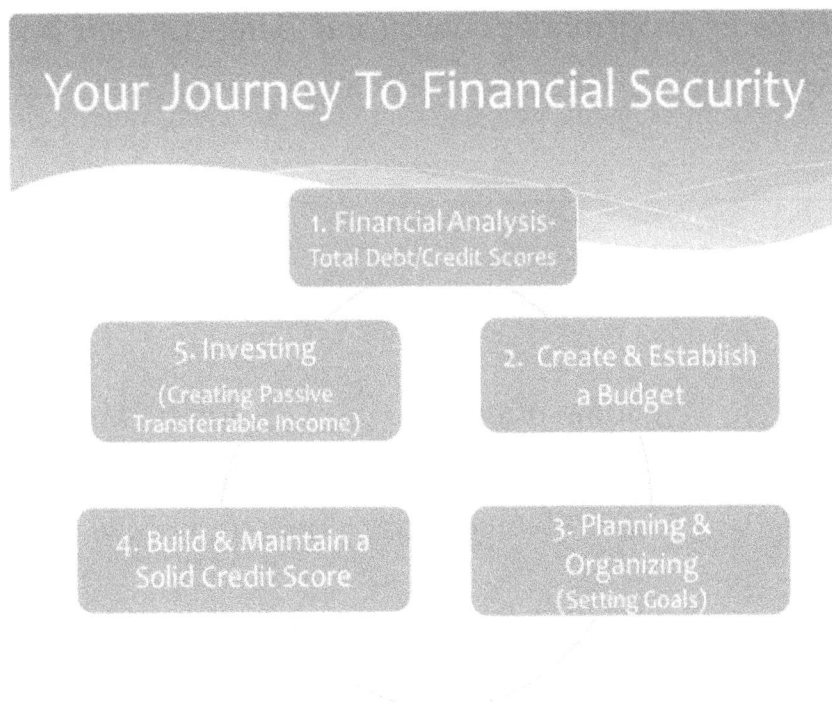

Your Journey To Financial Security

1. Financial Analysis- Total Debt/Credit Scores

5. Investing (Creating Passive Transferrable Income)

2. Create & Establish a Budget

4. Build & Maintain a Solid Credit Score

3. Planning & Organizing (Setting Goals)

What are your assumptions about money?

It's important to understand money, where our perceptions about money originated, and what tools you need to live a prosperous life. There are different levels of prosperity depending on the individual, but it was never the intention for anyone to be in survival mode living paycheck-to-paycheck.

Please keep an open mind when completing the following sections and be as accurate as you can with your answers.

Is having money a want or a necessity to living? _____

Write down 1-5 assumptions you have about money based on your answer above.

1. _____

2. _____

3. _____

4. _____

5. _____

Where does your belief about money come from? (parents, friend, books, television, self-taught)

_____

Is your belief about money accurate?

Yes _____, No _____, Some principles _____, I don't know _____

What is one thing you would change today concerning how you manage your **Money?**

_____

Money Management Questionnaire

Answer the following questions honestly: (Place a **Y** for Yes or **N** for No)

1. Do you currently have a savings account with at least 3-month surplus?
    _____

2. Are you currently debt free other than a mortgage for a home? _____

3. Do you have a credit score of 750 or greater? _____

4. Do you currently have a budget that you utilize to make personal financial decisions? _____

5. Do you currently have a legalized Will? _____

6. Do you currently have a Life Insurance policy that has an allotted amount to cover burial expenses, all financial obligations, and provides a surplus of funds for the remaining family members? _____

7. Do you have profitable investments that are transferrable as an inheritance?
    _____

If **all** your answers were **yes**, you are considered financially stable.

If **any** of your answers were **no**, please forget everything you learned about **Money** and open your mind to change, so you can see it from a different perspective other than your own and start your journey to financial success.

Is there anything wrong with desiring to have Money? No, not at all, because **money** is one of the most important resources you need in order to live. The key is not to become consumed with money, because it's greed that can lead to theft, improper solicitation of products & services, and strained relationships.

It's also imperative not to loan money you don't have, because if repayment is not made, it can cause a financial hardship or result in tense relationships. The same premise applies when it comes to co-signing for family and friends!

Other important money principles include having a will and adequate Life Insurance.

Why are Will's important?

It depicts a clear plan of how to distribute any property you own in the event of your death, it may also legally specify other provisions, including: Ensuring your spouse, partner, and/or children receives all your possessions without your estate being contested.

Do you currently have a Will? _____

In some instances, when people are asked if they have a will and the answer is "no", it's because they don't like the notion of planning for death. The harsh reality is everyone will eventually pass away, so why not have a clear plan of action to protect your wealth and legacy?

If your answer was no, what are the barriers that have kept you from composing a will?

Furthermore, are you willing to draft a will and get it notarized within the next 7 days?

The likelihood of you completing this task will diminish over time due to other conflicting priorities in life.

See a sample copy of a Last Will and Testament on the next page.

LAST WILL AND TESTAMENT OF JOHN DOE

I, John Doe, presently of York, Pennsylvania, declare that this is my Last Will and Testament.

PRELIMINARY DECLARATIONS

Prior Wills and Codicils

1. I revoke all prior Wills and Codicils.

Marital Status

2. I am married to Jane Doe.

Current Children

3. I have the following living children:

- Jimmy Doe; and

- Jill Doe.

4. The term 'child' or 'children' as used in this my Will includes the above listed children and any children of mine that are subsequently born or legally adopted.

EXECUTOR

Definition

5. The expression 'my Executor' used throughout this Will includes either the singular or plural number, or the masculine or feminine gender as appropriate wherever the fact or context so requires. The term 'executor' in this Will is synonymous with and includes the terms 'personal representative,' 'executrix,' and 'trustee.'

Appointment

6. I appoint my spouse, Jane Doe, as the sole Executor of this my Will, but if my spouse should predecease me, or should refuse or be unable to act or continue to act as my Executor, then I appoint Henry Doe of York, Pennsylvania to be the sole

Executor of this my Will in the place of my spouse.

7. No bond or other security of any kind will be required of any Executor appointed in this my Will.

Powers of My Executor

8. I give and appoint to my Executor the following duties and powers with respect to my estate:

a. To pay my legally enforceable debts, funeral expenses and all expenses in connection with the administration of my estate and the trusts created by my Will as soon as convenient after my death. If any of the real property devised in my Will remains subject to a mortgage at the time of my death, then I direct that the devisee taking that mortgaged property will take the property subject to that mortgage and that the devisee will not be entitled to have the mortgage paid out or resolved from the remaining assets of the residue of my estate;

b. To take all legal actions to have the probate of my Will completed as quickly and simply as possible, and as free as possible from any court supervision, under the laws of the Commonwealth of Pennsylvania;

c. To retain, exchange, insure, repair, improve, sell or dispose of any and all personal property belonging to my estate as my Executor deems advisable without liability for loss or depreciation;

d. To invest, manage, lease, rent, exchange, mortgage, sell, dispose of or give options without being limited as to term and to insure, repair, improve, or add to or otherwise deal with any and all real property belonging to my estate as my Executor deems advisable without liability for loss or depreciation;

e. To purchase, maintain, convert and liquidate investments or securities, and to vote stock, or exercise any option concerning any investments or securities without liability for loss;

f. To open or close bank accounts;

g. To maintain, continue, dissolve, change or sell any business which is part of my estate, or to purchase any business if deemed necessary or beneficial to my estate by my Executor;

h. To maintain, settle, abandon, sue or defend, or otherwise deal with any lawsuits against my estate;

i. To employ any lawyer, accountant or other professional; and

j. Except as otherwise provided in this my Will, to act as my Trustee by holding in trust the share of any minor beneficiary, and to keep such share invested, pay the income or capital or as much of either or both as my Executor considers advisable for the maintenance, education, advancement or benefit of such minor beneficiary and to pay or transfer the capital of such share or the amount remaining of that share to such beneficiary when he or she reaches the age of 25 years, or prior to such beneficiary reaching the age of 25 years, to pay or transfer such share to any parent or guardian of such beneficiary subject to like conditions and the receipt of any such parent or guardian discharges my Executor.

9. The above authority and powers granted to my Executor are in addition to any powers and elective rights conferred by state or federal law or by other provision of this Will and may be exercised as often as required, and without application to or approval by any court.

DISPOSITION OF ESTATE

Specific Bequests

10. To receive a specific bequest under this Will a beneficiary must survive me for thirty (30) days. Any item that fails to pass to a beneficiary will return to my estate to be included in the residue of my estate. All property given under this Will is subject to any encumbrances or liens attached to the property. My specific bequests are as follows:

a. I leave to Lenny Doe of York, Pennsylvania, if they shall survive me, for their own use absolutely, the following: My coin collection.

Distribution of Residue

11. To receive any gift or property under this Will a beneficiary must survive me for thirty (30) days. Beneficiaries of my estate residue will receive and share all of my property and assets not specifically bequeathed or otherwise required for the payment of any debts owed, including but not limited to, expenses associated with the probate of my Will, the payment of taxes, funeral expenses or any other expense resulting from the administration of my Will. The entire estate residue is to be divided between my designated beneficiaries with the beneficiaries receiving a share of the entire estate residue. All property given under this Will is subject to any encumbrances or liens attached to the property.

12. The entire residue of my estate will be transferred to my spouse, if my spouse survives me for thirty (30) full days, for their own use absolutely.

13. If my spouse is not living on the thirtieth day following my death, I direct my Executor to divide the residue of my estate into as many equal shares as there shall be children of mine then alive at my death, subject to the provisions hereinafter specified and to pay and transfer one such share to each of those surviving children. If any child of mine shall die before becoming entitled, in accordance with the terms of this my Will, to receive the whole of his or her share of my estate, but such child has a child or children which survive me, that child of mine shall be deemed to have survived me for the purposes of this division and the share of that child of mine or the amount remaining thereof shall be distributed according to the provisions hereinafter provided.

14. If any child of mine shall die before becoming entitled in accordance with the terms of this my Will, to receive the whole of his or her share of my estate, I direct that such share or the amount remaining of that share will be divided and transferred in equal shares to each of the surviving children of that deceased child of mine. And if any of such children of my deceased child dies before receiving the whole of his or her share of my estate, that share or the amount remaining

thereof will be divided in equal shares amongst the surviving children of that child of mine. But if that deceased child of mine leaves no surviving children, then that share or the amount remaining of that share will be divided amongst my surviving children in equal shares.

Wipeout Provision

15. Should my spouse predecease me, or fail to survive me for thirty (30) full days and should I leave no children, child, grandchildren or grandchild surviving me, or should they all die before becoming entitled to receive the whole of their share of my estate, then I direct my Executor to divide any remaining residue of my estate into one hundred (100) equal shares and to pay and transfer such shares as follows:

a. 50 shares to be divided equally between my parents and siblings, or the survivors thereof, for their own use absolutely, if all or any of them is then alive. If any of these beneficiaries shall die before becoming entitled, in accordance with the terms of this my Will, to receive the whole of his or her share of my estate, but such beneficiary has a child or children which survive me, that beneficiary shall be deemed to have survived me for the purposes of this distribution. Provided however, that if all of my parents and siblings shall predecease me and have no children surviving them, or surviving me, die before receiving their share of my estate, I direct that their share of my estate or the amount remaining of that share will be divided equally between my spouse's parents and siblings for their own use absolutely, if all or any of them is then alive; and

b. 50 shares to be divided equally between my spouse's parents and siblings, or the survivors thereof, for their own use absolutely, if all or any of them is then alive. If any of these beneficiaries shall die before becoming entitled, in accordance with the terms of this my Will, to receive the whole of his or her share of my estate, but such beneficiary has a child or children which survive me, that beneficiary shall be deemed to have survived me for the purposes of this distribution. Provided however, that if all of my spouse's parents and siblings shall predecease me and have no children surviving them, or surviving me, die before receiving their share of my estate, I direct that their share of my estate or the amount remaining of that share will be divided equally between my parents and siblings for their own use absolutely, if all or any of them is then alive.

CHILDREN

Guardian for Minor and Dependent Children

16. Should my Spouse not survive me and should my minor or dependent children require a guardian to care for them, I appoint the following individual to be their guardian (the 'Guardian'):

a. I appoint Debbie Doe of York, Pennsylvania to be the sole Guardian of all my minor and dependent children until they are at least 18 years of age.

TESTAMENTARY TRUST

Testamentary Trust for Minor Beneficiaries

17. It is my intent to create a testamentary trust (the "Testamentary Trust") for each minor beneficiary named in this my Will. I name my Executor(s) as trustee (the "Trustee") of any and all Testamentary Trusts required in this my Will. Any assets bequeathed, transferred, or gifted to a minor beneficiary named in this my Will are to be held in a separate trust by the Trustee until that minor beneficiary reaches the designated age. Any property left by me to any minor beneficiary in this my Will shall be given to my Executor(s) to be managed until that minor beneficiary reaches the age of 25.

Trust Administration

18. The Trustee shall manage the Testamentary Trust as follows:

1.   The assets and property will be managed for the benefit of the minor until the minor reaches the age set by me for final distribution;

2.   Upon the minor reaching the age set by me for final distribution, all property and assets remaining in the trust will be transferred to the minor beneficiary as

quickly as possible; and

3.   Until the minor beneficiary reaches the age set by me for final distribution, my Trustee will keep the assets of the trust invested and pay the whole or such part of the net income derived therefrom and any amount or amounts out of the capital that my Trustee may deem advisable to or for the support, health, maintenance, education, or benefit of that minor beneficiary.

19.   The Trustee may, in the Trustee's discretion, invest and reinvest trust funds in any kind of real or personal property and any kind of investment, provided that the Trustee acts with the care, skill, prudence and diligence, considering all financial and economic considerations, that a prudent person acting in a similar capacity and familiar with such matters would use.

20.   No bond or other security of any kind will be required of any Trustee appointed in this my Will.

Trust Termination

21.   The Testamentary Trust will end after any of the following:

A.   The minor beneficiary reaching the age set by me for final distribution;

B.   The minor beneficiary dies; or

C.   The assets of the trust are exhausted through distributions.

General Trust Provisions

22. The expression 'my Trustee' used throughout this Will includes either the singular or plural number, or the masculine or feminine gender as appropriate wherever the fact or context so requires.

(1) Powers of Trustee

To carry out the terms of my Will, I give my Trustee the following powers to be used in his or her discretion at any time in the management of a trust created hereunder, namely:

A.   The power to make such expenditures as are necessary to carry out the purpose of the trust;

B.   Subject to my express direction to the contrary, the power to sell, call in and convert into money any trust property, including real property, that my Trustee in his or her discretion deems advisable;

C.   Subject to my express direction to the contrary, the power to mortgage trust property where my Trustee considers it advisable to do so;

D.   Subject to my express direction to the contrary, the power to borrow money where my Trustee considers it advisable to do so;

E.   Subject to my express direction to the contrary, the power to lend money to the trust beneficiary if my Trustee considers it is in the best interest of the beneficiary to do so;

F.   To make expenditures for the purpose of repairing, improving and rebuilding any property;

G.   To exercise all rights and options of an owner of any securities held in trust;

H.   To lease trust property, including real estate, without being limited as to term;

I.   To make investments he or she considers advisable, without being limited to those investments authorized by law for trustees;

J.   To receive additional property from any source and in any form of ownership;

K.   Instead of acting personally, to employ and pay any other person or persons, including a body corporate, to transact any business or to do any act of any nature in relation to a trust created under my Will including the receipt and payment of money, without being liable for any loss incurred. And I authorize my Trustee to appoint from time to time upon such terms as he or she may think fit any person or persons, including a body corporate, for the purpose of exercising any powers herein expressly or impliedly given to my Trustee with respect to any property belonging to the trust;

L.   Without the consent of any persons interested in trusts established hereunder, to compromise, settle or waive any claim or claims at any time due to or by the trust in such manner and to such extent as my Trustee considers to be in the best interest of the trust beneficiary, and to make an agreement with any other person, persons or corporation in respect thereof, which shall be binding upon such beneficiary;

M.   To make or not make any election, determination, designation or allocation required or permitted to be made by my Trustee (either alone or jointly with others) under any of the provisions of any local, state, federal, or other taxing statute, in such manner as my Trustee, in his or her absolute discretion, deems advisable, and each such election, determination, designation or allocation when so made shall be final and binding upon all persons concerned;

N.   To pay himself or herself a reasonable compensation out of the trust assets; and

O.   To employ and rely on the advice given by any attorney, accountant, investment advisor, or other agent to assist the Trustee in the administration of this trust and to compensate them from the trust assets.

The above authority and powers granted to my Trustee are in addition to any powers and elective rights conferred by statute or federal law or by other provision of this Will and may be exercised as often as required, and without application to or approval by any court.

(2) Other Provisions

A. Subject to the terms of this my Will, I direct that my Trustee will not be liable for any loss to my estate or to any beneficiary resulting from the exercise by him or her in good faith of any discretion given him or her in this my Will;

B. Any trust created in this Will shall be administered as independently of court supervision as possible under the laws of the State having jurisdiction over the trust; and

C. If any trust condition is held invalid, it will not affect other provisions that can be given effect without the invalid provision.

GENERAL PROVISIONS

Individuals Omitted from Bequests

23. If I have omitted to leave property in this Will to one or more of my heirs as named above or have provided them with zero shares of a bequest, the failure to do so is intentional.

Insufficient Estate

24. If the value of my estate is insufficient to fulfill all of the bequests described in this Will, then I give my Executor full authority to decrease each bequest by a proportionate amount.

No Contest Provision

If any beneficiary under this Will contests in any court any of the provisions of this Will, then each and all such persons shall not be entitled to any devises, legacies, bequests, or benefits under this Will or any codicil hereto, and such interest or share in my estate shall be disposed of as if that contesting beneficiary had not survived me.

Severability

If any provisions of this Will are deemed unenforceable, the remaining provisions will remain in full force and effect.

IN WITNESS WHEREOF, I have signed my name on this the 3rd day of January, 2019, at York, Pennsylvania, declaring and publishing this instrument as my Last Will, in the presence of the undersigned witnesses, who witnessed and subscribed this Last Will at my request, and in my presence.

_____

John Doe (Testator) Signature

SIGNED AND DECLARED by John Doe on the 3rd day of January, 2019 to be the Testator's Last Will, in our presence, at York, Pennsylvania, who at the Testator's request and in the presence of the Testator and of each other, all being present at the same time, have signed our names as witnesses.

_____   _____

Witness #1 Signature   Witness #2 Signature

_____   _____

Witness #1 Name (Please Print)   Witness #2 Name (Please Print)

_____   _____

Witness #1 Street Address   Witness #2 Street Address

_____   _____

Witness #1 City/State   Witness #2 City/State

AFFIDAVIT

STATE OF PENNSYLVANIA

COUNTY OF _____

I, John Doe, the Testator, sign my name to this instrument this _____ day of _____, 20_____, and being first duly sworn, declare to the undersigned authority all of the following:

1. I execute this instrument as my Last Will.
2. I sign this Last Will willingly, or willingly direct another to sign for me.
3. I execute this Last Will as my free and voluntary act for the purposes expressed therein.
4. I am 18 years of age or older, of sound mind and under no constraint or undue influence.

Testator: _____

We, _____, _____ and _____, the witnesses, being first duly sworn, sign our names to this instrument and declare to the undersigned authority all of the following:

1. The Testator executes this instrument as their Last Will.
2. The Testator signs it willingly, or willingly directs another to sign for them.
3. Each of us, in the conscious presence of the Testator, signs this Last Will as a witness.
4. To the best of our knowledge, the Testator is 18 years of age or older, of sound mind and under no constraint or undue influence.

_____   _____
Witness #1   Witness #2

Subscribed and sworn to before me by John Doe, the Testator, and by _____, _____ and _____, witnesses, this _____ day of _____, 20_____.

(Seal)

(Signed) _____

_____

(Official capacity of officer)

©2002-2019 LawDepot.com®

Why do you need to have adequate Life Insurance?

1. Protect your family and loved ones

   - If your loved ones depend on your financial support for their livelihood, then life insurance is a must, because it replaces your income when you die.

2. To pay off debts and other expenses

   - In addition to providing income to cover everyday living expenses, your family needs insurance to cover any outstanding debts, like the mortgage, credit cards and car loans. Other expenses include funeral and burial costs that can easily run into the tens of thousands of dollars. You don't want your spouse, parents, children or other loved ones to be left with any financial burdens in addition to the emotional stress they're already suffering.

3. To leave an inheritance

   - Even if you don't have any other assets to pass to your heirs, you can create an inheritance by buying a Life Insurance policy and naming them as beneficiaries.

Do you currently have Life Insurance? _____

If you answered yes, do you have enough Life Insurance to cover your family's needs and give them financial security and peace of mind? _____

If the answer is no to either one of these questions, get with a Life Insurance agent immediately or check into your benefits on the job about a policy that meets your financial obligations and needs.

Notes:

Key Points:

_____

_____

_____

_____

_____

_____

_____

How can I apply this in my life?

_____

_____

_____

_____

Action plan or next steps:

_____

_____

_____

_____

_____

Chapter 1
Financial Analysis

"I believe that through knowledge and discipline, financial peace is possible for all of us."

Dave Ramsey

FINANCIAL ANALYSIS

Financial analysis is concerned with understanding the personal resources available by examining net worth and household cash flows. Net worth is a person's balance sheet, calculated by adding up all assets under that person's control, minus all liabilities of the household, at one point in time. Household cash flows total up all from the expected sources of income within a year, minus all expected expenses within the same year. From this analysis, you can determine to what degree and in what time the personal goals can be accomplished.

This is the first step to changing your financial position. You can't change what you don't know. I remember the first time I completed my net worth worksheet. I was a homeowner with approximately twenty-thousand dollars ($20,000) worth of equity, which was pretty good at the time considering it only had been 2 years. I had a few other assets that was worth about fifteen thousand dollars ($15,000) and a savings account with eleven thousand ($11,000) dollars. Considering I was in my early thirties at the time, forty-six thousand dollars ($46,000) in assets was pretty good. The problem was I had fifty-eight thousand dollars ($58,000) in liabilities, most of it coming from credit card debt. I know, "Wow!" I said the same thing. This was the hardest part of the process. I had an idea that my financial state was bad, but you really don't fully grasp the situation until you can visualize it on paper. I took a deep breath, said to myself, "It is what it is," and realized the only thing left to do now is to prepare my plan and take it one day at a time.

Now that I have shared with you my starting point, I hope I have eased your mind or any concerns you may have about going forward with this process. I wasn't always financially savvy. Most people become experts in their fields because of failures they have experienced.

I love this quote by Will Smith; **"Failure is a massive part of being able to become successful."**

It's not about where you are today, but the journey you are willing to take going forward.

Financial Analysis

On the next page is a net worth calculation sheet. Take your time completing the analysis because you want your information to be as accurate as possible. There are tools online that you can utilize to determine the value of your possessions. While some assets will have very specific and obvious values (such as your bank statements or IRA's), others will require you to make an estimate. Sites like Zillow or Redfin offer estimated home values, and while they shouldn't be taken too literally, they can give you a ballpark idea of what your home is worth. You can also get an appraisal done for a minimal fee or have a realtor do a CMA (Comparable Market Analysis) on your home, at no cost, to give you an estimate value. Kelley Blue Book or Edmunds can help you determine the value of your car, motorcycle, or boat. By looking up comparable items on a resale site like eBay, it can help you gauge the real value of other random items like jewelry, art, or rare coins. If you run into any walls, feel free to reach out to any financial advisor for assistance.

Net Worth Calculation Worksheet

An important step in gaining financial control is to calculate your net worth (assets – debts). Every year, your net worth should be tabulated in review of your progress and compare it with financial goals.

Assets (What You Own)
Cash:
Cash On-Hand $_____

Checking Account $_____

Savings Account $_____

Money Market Funds $_____

Cash Value of Life Insurance $_____

Other $_____

Real Estate/Property:
Home $_____

Land $_____

Other $_____

Investments: (Market Value)
Certificates of Deposit $_____

Stocks $_____

Bonds $_____

Mutual Funds $_____

Annuities $_____

IRAs $_____

401 (K), 403 (B), 457 Plans $_____

Other $_____

Personal Property: (Present Value)
Automobiles $_____

Recreational Vehicle/Boat $_____

Home Furnishings $_____

Appliances and Furniture $_____

Jewelry and Furs $_____

Other $_____

Total Assets $_____

Liabilities (What You Owe)
Current Debts:
Household $_____

Medical $_____

Credit Cards $_____

Department Store Cards $_____

Back Taxes $_____

Legal $_____

Other $_____

Mortgages:
Home $_____

Land $_____

Other $_____

Loans:
Bank/Finance Companies $_____

Automobiles $_____

Recreational Vehicle/Boat $_____

Educational $_____

Life Insurance $_____

Personal $_____

Other $_____

Total Liabilities $_____

Net Worth $_____

Financial Analysis

Ok, breathe. What were your results? Remember, I shared with you that I had a net worth of a negative twelve thousand dollars ($12,000), so it's just the beginning.

The next step in your financial evaluation is a credit analysis. You need to review your credit report, so you know your score. Chapter four will go into greater detail about credit, so don't worry about results at this time.

There are several search engines you can use to pull your credit score. There are some that are free, but the information is not as accurate as third-party companies that specialize in providing this type of data.

I personally have been using privacyguard.com since 2006 because of the benefits associated with this credit monitoring company.

What is your score? _____

The second part of the financial analysis is evaluating how your home's cash flows total up from the expected sources of income within a year, minus all expected expenses within the same year.

The best way to review this is by completing a budget, which will be discussed in the next chapter.

Notes:

Key Points:

_____

_____

_____

_____

_____

_____

_____

_____

How can I apply this in my life?

_____

_____

_____

_____

_____

Action plan or next steps:

_____

_____

_____

_____

_____

Chapter 2
Planning the Budget

"A budget is telling your money where to go instead of wondering where it went."
David Ramsey

BUDGETING

What is a budget?

A budget is a financial plan for spending money. It's a tool that you can use to feel more in control of your finances, because you are able to allocate your income-to-debt ratio, household expenses, and/or a savings account.

How can a budget help you?

A budget helps individuals manage their spending and arrange their expenditures, so short- or long-term goals like eliminating debt or retiring early can be achieved.

What are the benefits to budgeting?

There are numerous benefits to budgeting. A good budget enables you to plan and save for large purchases by controlling daily expenses. Budgeting allows you to avoid spending unnecessarily, because you know exactly what items you are purchasing. In addition, a budget provides early warnings of potential problems in advance, so you can adjust. Finally, if you are budgeting effectively, it will create financial stability and peace of mind.

There are many types of budgets that help people from all walks of life. Budgets should be simple, flexible and have purpose and defined goals that is achieved within a certain time period.

The process of creating a budget is just as critical as the execution of a budget. You need to know your total income, how much you owe, any recurring variable expenses, and due dates. Follow the steps on the next page to get your budget started.

Budgeting

Step I - Get online and obtain the last six (6) months of your billing information for bills such as your home phone, cell phone, cable, energy, gas, sewage, water, insurance, mortgage/rent, car or truck note, credit cards and loans, etc.

Find out the due dates for your fixed bills and get a rough estimate for the bills that change from month-to-month.

Most banks will have 3-to-6 months history online. If your bank doesn't, you can call them and request copies of your statements and have them mailed to your house.

Step II - Take all your bills and create an excel spreadsheet and break them out in the following six categories:

1. Bank Information
   - Institution name, phone #, bank routing #, savings account #, checking account #, debit card #, web address
2. Mortgage/Rental Home Information
   - Creditor name, address, phone #, loan or account # website address
3. Vehicle Loans
   - Creditor name, address, phone #, loan/account #, VIN #, website address
4. Credit Card/Installment Loans
   - Credit card name, address, phone #, card account or loan #, card expiration date and 3-digit pin (CVV), website address
5. Utilities Information
   - Merchant name, address, phone #, customer service hours, account #, website address
6. Car/Home/Life Insurance Information
   - Company name, address, phone #, claims agent name, policy #, website address

If you have all your information in one centralized location, it will make it easier to obtain when you need to contact the merchants or make changes to your account.

Step III - Total up your monthly income (salary, investments, child support) and input the data into the designated space.

Step IV - Input your expenses into the projected monthly payment section of the spreadsheet. Be as accurate as possible. Look at your bank statements and gage how much you think you spend on your miscellaneous bills.

(See an example of a monthly budget sheet on the next page)

Step V - After entering all your information, you will discover the most important number in the budgeting process—**the bottom line**. This number will tell you whether you are overspending. Ultimately, during this step, you will determine if you are living within or beyond your means. If the bottom line of your budget shows you are overspending, the most difficult step is next—making cuts to your monthly expenses based on your obligations. Make sure your adjustments are based upon reality and flexible or you will stop the process out of frustration. Page 13 will outline some tips you can take to reduce your spending. Ideally, your budget should be set up, so your spending aligns with the 50/20/30 rule. The basic rule is to divide after-tax income, spending 50% on needs and 30% on wants while allocating 20% to savings or investments.

Needs are those bills that you absolutely must pay and are the things necessary for survival. These include rent or mortgage payments, car payments, groceries, insurance, healthcare, minimum debt payment and utilities.

Wants are all the things you spend money on that are not essential. This includes dinner and movies out, that new handbag, tickets to sporting events, vacations, or the latest electronics gadget. This category also includes those upgrade decisions you make, such as buying a high-end car instead of a more economical vehicle. Basically, wants are all those little extras you spend money on that make life more enjoyable and entertaining.

There is an example of a percentage (%) based-budget on the following page to assist you.

MONTHLY BUDGET SHEET	BUDGET	ACTUAL
BEGINNING BALANCE		$
INCOME		
	$	$
	$	$
	$_____	$_____
TOTAL MONTHLY INCOME	$	$
EXPENSES		
House		
Mortgage/Rent	$	$
Home/Renter's Insurance	$	$
Utilities		
Gas	$	$
Energy	$	$
Cable	$	$
Home Phone	$	$
Cell Phone	$	$
Water	$	$
Automobiles		
Car Note	$	$
Car Note	$	$
Car Insurance (s)		
	$	$
	$	$
Personal Loans		
	$	$
	$	$
Credit Card(s)		
	$	$
	$	$
	$	$
Miscellaneous Bills		
Tithes/Offerings	$	$
Car and Home Repairs and Upkeep	$	$
Medicine/Health	$	$
Federal or State Taxes	$	$
Gas/Food/Entertainment		
Gas	$	$
Groceries	$	$
Clothes/Appearance/Apparel	$	$
Entertainment: Food/Vacation/Movies/etc.	$_____	$_____
TOTAL EXPENSES	$	$
ENDING BALANCE	$	$

% Based Budget

50/30/20

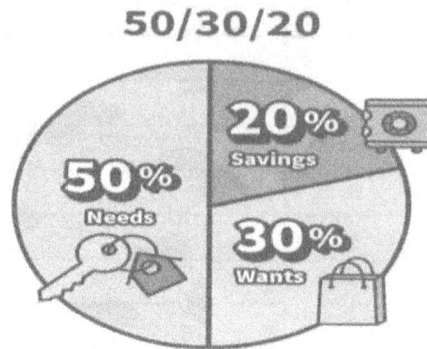

Monthly net pay is $5,000 and you follow 50/30/20 rule, 50% or $2,500 for these necessities:

- $950 for rent/mortgage
- $300 for utilities (gas, electric, water, sewage) (Household expenses should not exceed 25%)
- $300 for your car payment
- $100 for car insurance
- $400 for groceries
- $250 for loans
- $200 for misc (medical, car or home repair)

30% or $1,500 towards your personal expenses

- dining out
- shopping
- your cable or cell phone plan
- travel or leisure expenses
- gift spending or a gym membership

20% or $1,000 towards your savings or investing
This could be anything from a simple deposit account to a rainy-day fund or contributing to an investment account.

As I stated in step V of the budgeting process, your budget should be flexible enough, so you can adjust to your current conditions. Going forward, your financial goals should align with the terminology above, so you are making sound monetary decisions.

Budgeting

"It's not your salary that makes you rich, it's your spending habits."

Here are 15 tips to cut expenses:

1. If you are grocery shopping, always make a list of essential items. Do not shop on an empty stomach or you will buy things that look good at that moment.
2. Shop at discount stores or wholesale outlets.
3. Use the internet to shop because you will avoid impulse purchases if you go to the mall or shopping center.
4. Don't just clip coupons, use them!
5. Scale back on shopping for brand name items versus store brands.
6. Scale back on the number of times you go to the nail or hair salon/barbershop, and/or car wash. Wash your own car.
7. Shop around and negotiate lower rates on credit cards, auto or homeowner's insurance.
8. Eliminate late fees or ATM fees. Every bank has other banks they are affiliated with where there will be no service charges. Every dollar spent in a day adds up to $365.00 dollars a year.
9. Reduce your cable bill by limiting your package selection to your favorite channels.
10. Reduce eating out every day to two days a week. Cook extra food and take it for lunch, so you don't have to leave out and buy food.
11. Always examine your bills, especially cell phone bills, to make sure they are correct and you are not overbilled.
12. Buy generic medicines.
13. Stop buying magazines and newspapers and utilize the internet or the local library.
14. Alter your movie-going experience. Watch movies at home versus the movie theatre.
15. Carpool when possible.

Budgeting

Step VI - Keeping track of your budget takes an hour or so a week. Once you have created a budget, you want to stay on top of it. This requires discipline to the process and committing time to input your information as well as the buy-in and support from family members.

Step VII - Creating Budget goals.

» I/We agree to live on a budget.

» I/We agree to balance our checkbook to the penny every month.

» I/We agree to create a goal of setting aside three months income for an emergency surplus fund.

» If I/We use credit cards, I/We agree to pay off the balances each month or stop using the cards altogether.

» I/We agree to live within our means.

» I/We agree to save something every month.

» I/We agree to give to local charities or organizations that support the community.

Signature: _____

Signature: _____

In conclusion, the discipline of applying this information will empower you to make sound short- and long-term financial decisions and will provide you with a great deal of comfort. You will see positive results for your sacrifice and begin to live life prosperously and not survive paycheck-to-paycheck.

Today, I religiously update my budget daily. It is apart of what I do without thinking about it. Keep pushing yourself every day until it becomes a way of life for you. Also, understand that personal budgets are designed to be flexible, so continue to adjust as necessary.

Notes:

Key Points:

_____

_____

_____

_____

_____

_____

_____

_____

_____

How can I apply this in my life?

_____

_____

_____

_____

_____

Action plan or next steps:

_____

_____

_____

_____

_____

This page was intentionally left blank

CHAPTER 3
Planning

"Planning and then executing are necessary to reach any goal in life."

Sabrina Quairoli

PLANNING AND ORGANIZING

Why is planning your path financially important?

You must have a well-thought-out, logical, and reasonable plan to get from where you are now to where you want to be.

The first step is to set goals. Goals are like targets; they give you something to aim for. When you set a goal for yourself, you make a commitment to do something. By doing it, you step out onto a path toward change.

First, figure out what you want to achieve most in your life. This can range from buying a house to starting a business or retiring according to your own schedule. Without goals, any money you earn can easily be spent instead of being saved or earmarked for an important milestone or goal. As well as identifying financial goals, estimate the amount of money you'll need to accumulate to reach each your goal.

There are three types of goals: short, intermediate and long term.

1. Short-term goals are those you plan to accomplish within a year.
2. Intermediate goals are those you plan to accomplish within one to five years
3. Long-term goals have a time frame of five years and beyond.

Examples of short-term goals:
- Eliminate credit card debt
- Set up a rainy-day fund
- Adjust your spending habits

Examples of intermediate goals:
- Purchase a home
- Buy a new car
- Change jobs

Planning and Organizing

Examples of long-term goals:

- Pay off your mortgage early
- College fund for your children
- Early retirement

Each type of goals should be written down and reviewed daily. When you write down your goals, you increase your commitment to them, and when you review them often, you work them into your subconscious, so they become a part of you.

Every goal you set should be realistic, measurable, and flexible. It's important to be realistic when setting goals so that you can enjoy the satisfaction of success rather than the heartbreak of underachievement. Goals should be measurable so that you can objectively tell whether they've been met. They should not conflict with other goals, and they should be flexible enough to change if your circumstances change.

For example, I set a goal one year to pay down ten thousand dollars ($10,000) in debt, while saving 10% of my earnings. In November of that year, I achieved both my financial goals, so I rewarded myself with a trip to Jamaica for Christmas. As you are setting goals, it's also important to celebrate milestones, so you remain motivated.

At this point in the workbook, you should have completed your net worth calculation worksheet, pulled your credit report (so you know your score), and established a budget. Now it's time for you to complete the personal financial goals worksheet. Utilize the "Setting Financial Goals" worksheet on the next page as a guide to assist you in developing your financial goals.

Setting Financial Goals Worksheet

The number of goals you set is up to you. It is helpful to estimate as best you can the time frame for each goal and the amount of money involved based on your lifestyle. Be as specific as possible.

Goal	Short-term ((6 Months to 1 Year)	Intermediate (1 to 5 Years)	Long-Term (5 Years and Beyond)
Relgiious/Charitable Giving	$	$	$
Build up emergency reserve	$	$	$
Achieve adequate Retirement Income (401(k), IRA)	$	$	$
Buy adequate Insurance	$	$	$
Pay off Credit Cards	$	$	$
Create a College Fund	$	$	$
Buy a car	$	$	$
Save down payment for House	$	$	$
Make home improvements	$	$	$
Pay off Mortgage early	$	$	$
Take a vacation	$	$	$
Start a Business	$	$	$
Change Jobs	$	$	$
Take early retirement	$	$	$
Help finance a family member	$	$	$
Other	N/A	N/A	N/A
	$	$	$
	$	$	$
	$	$	$

Personal Financial Goals Worksheet

Goal-setting is a powerful exercise. **"A goal without a plan is just a wish."** When you write down your plans, they have a way of becoming reality. This worksheet will help you define what's important to you.

Immediate or Short-Term Goals (six months to one year):

1. _____
2. _____
3. _____
4. _____

Intermediate Long-Term Goals (one to five years):

1. _____
2. _____
3. _____
4. _____

Long-Term Goals (Five years and beyond):

1. _____
2. _____
3. _____
4. _____

What's most Important? List your three most important goals:

1. _____
2. _____
3. _____

Personal Financial Goals Worksheet (Con't)

What could get in my way? List some obstacles to accomplishing your goals:

1. _____

2. _____

3. _____

What resources/tools do you need to accomplish your goals?

1. _____

2. _____

3. _____

Who can help me? List family members, friends, and/or professional(s)?

1. _____

2. _____

3. _____

When do I start?

Goal	Start date	End date
_____	_____	_____
_____	_____	_____
_____	_____	_____
_____	_____	_____
_____	_____	_____

After you complete this exercise, keep it in a safe place. Spend at least 10 minutes each morning planning how to translate your goals into action steps. When you make a regular habit of reviewing your goals, you will be better able to achieve them.

CHAPTER 4
Good Credit Matters

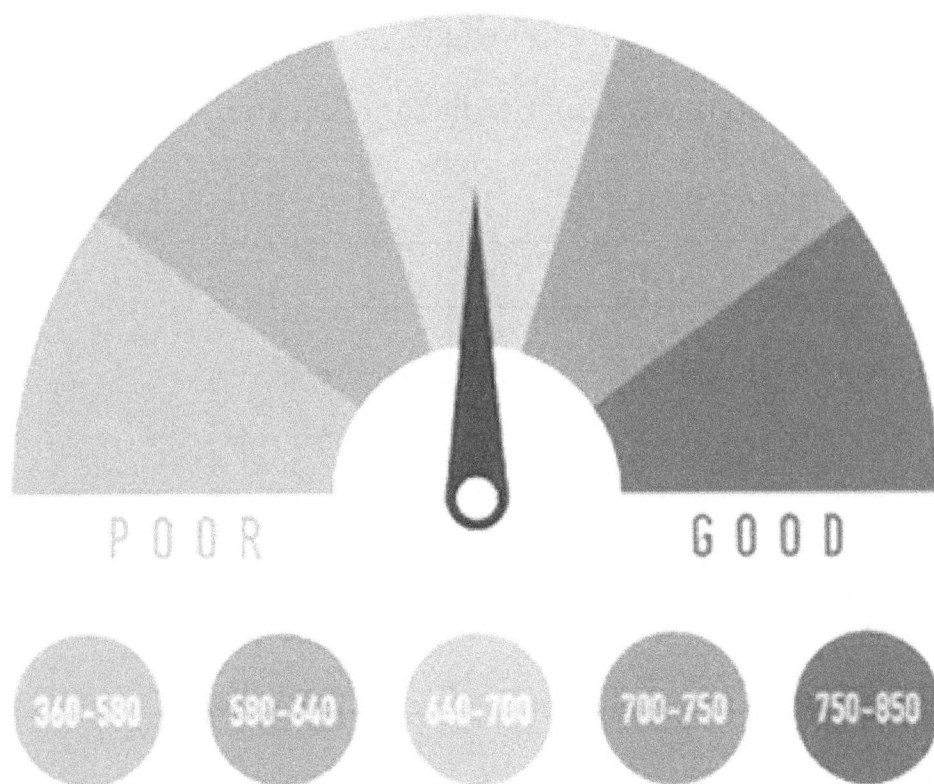

POOR   GOOD

360-580   580-640   640-700   700-750   750-850

"Your credit score doesn't measure wealth or success. It only measures your relationship with debt."
Unknown Source

Credit

What is Credit?

Credit is the ability of a customer to obtain goods or services before payment, based on the trust that payment will be made in the future.

Is having good Credit a want or a necessity to living? _____

Write down 1-5 assumptions you have about Credit based on your answer above.

1. _____
2. _____
3. _____
4. _____
5. _____

Where does your belief about Credit come from? (parents, friend, books, tv, self-taught)

_____

Based on knowledge passed down to me from my grandfather, I grew up believing that if I paid all my bills on time, my credit score would be good. To a small extent that is true, because slow pays drastically affects your score. However, there are other aspects that go into having excellent credit. Unfortunately, I didn't realize this was true until I went to Best Buy to purchase a television on credit and was denied. By law, if you are declined, the company/merchant must provide a reason in writing for your denial. I was rejected because my debt-to-income ratio was too high. If I would have pulled my credit report on a regular basis, I would have known my score was a 618 at the time, which is considered poor credit. This is a good lead to my next question for you.

Credit

Do you know your Credit score? _____

What are some of the benefits of having good credit?

1. Good credit gives you **purchasing power** to negotiate the amount of money you can borrow at the lowest rates for financing.
2. Obtain certain insurance coverages.
3. Securing employment because some jobs are requiring individuals to have certain credit scores to work for their organizations.

Is having credit cards bad? _____

If your answer is no, you are correct. Utilized properly, credit cards are a valuable source to manage spending, build your credit score and receive cash back rewards to spend at your discretion.

However, it is important to know the annual fee, finance/APR charge, interest on purchases and cash advances, and late and over-the-limit fees.

I heard someone say that "Credit Card companies are crooks." When I asked why they felt that way, they expressed how they received credit cards, but didn't know the interest rate was in the high 20's. By law, this information must be provided in the packet of information you receive with the card. Before you activate it, please familiarize yourself with the terms and conditions, so you don't fall into the trap of using a bad credit card that's going to cost you more debt in the end.

Now let's get started understanding about credit scores, how your credit score is calculated, what is a credit report and how to read it, and the steps that should be taken to build, monitor and maintain a strong credit rating.

What is a credit score?

Your credit score is a numerical value based on the information in your credit report. However, this number is separate from your credit report.

The scores are comprised of the following:

- Payment history
- Amount owed in relation to available credit
- Length of credit history
- New credit obtained
- Types of credit used

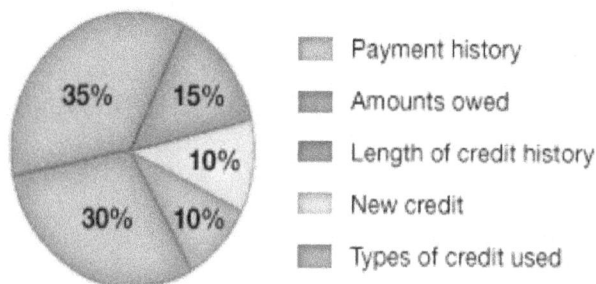

Payment history	
Amounts owed	
Length of credit history	
New credit	
Types of credit used	

How is your score calculated?

Equifax, Experian, Trans Union are the three main credit bureaus.

A credit repository is an agency that compiles data provided by creditors on the credit histories of individuals and distributes reports to potential creditors upon request.

A credit bureau is a local company that purchases data from a credit repository and makes it available to individuals and businesses.

Credit scores fall within a range of 300 to 850. Although lenders set their own basis for what is a "good" or "bad" credit score, below is a breakdown of credit score ranges:

- **Excellent Credit: 750+**
- **Good Credit: 700-749**
- **Fair/Average Credit: 650-699**
- **Poor Credit: 600-649**
- **Bad Credit: below 600**

Understanding credit ratings: how your credit gets a score

Most people are aware that you need a good (or at least decent) credit rating to get credit cards, a mortgage or other lines of credit. But if you have no credit history, you may not have a credit score.

Not all credit scores are the same. There are different scoring models, including Vantage Score® and FICO™. Fair, Isaac, and Company, Inc or better known as "FICO" score is the most well-known of the two. "FICO" developed a computerized scoring system that takes factors and predicts the possible occurrence of default. FICO credit scores are used by over 90% of lenders when it comes to providing you with a loan and when they grant the interest rates, terms and whether you are approved or not.

Although each system has its own formulas to calculate credit scores, there are some basic similarities.

Most credit scoring includes the following:

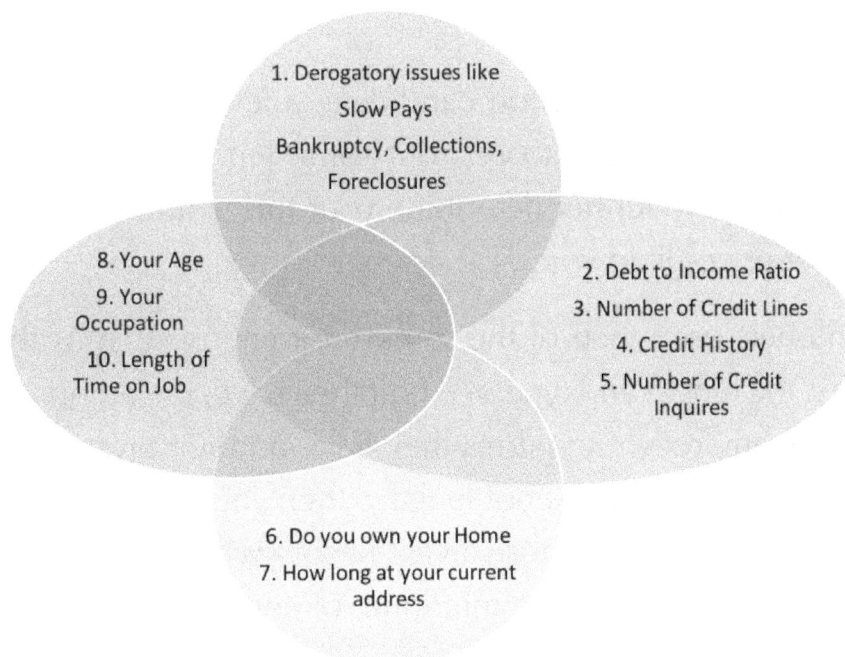

1. Derogatory issues like Slow Pays Bankruptcy, Collections, Foreclosures

8. Your Age
9. Your Occupation
10. Length of Time on Job

2. Debt to Income Ratio
3. Number of Credit Lines
4. Credit History
5. Number of Credit Inquires

6. Do you own your Home
7. How long at your current address

Credit scoring, including the FICO score and Vantage Score, operate within the range of 300 to 850, and a score of **700** or above is generally considered to be good. Within that range, there are different categories, from bad to excellent.

But even these aren't set in stone. Again, that's because lenders all have their own definitions of what is a good credit score. One lender that is looking to approve more borrowers might approve applicants with credit scores of 680 or higher. Another might be more selective and only approve those with scores of 750 or higher. Or both lenders might offer credit to anyone with a score of at least 650, but charge consumers with scores below 700 a higher interest rate!

But trying to pin down a specific number that means your credit score is **"good"** can be tricky. After all, there are lots of different credit scores that lenders use when trying to decide whether to grant you a loan. What one lender may view as a "good" score may fall into another lender's "fair" credit category.

What is a Vantage Score?

A Vantage Score is a credit scoring model that emerged over a decade ago and was a joint venture between Experian, Transunion, and Equifax. The Vantage Score model is used in comparison and competes with the Fair, Isaac and Company (FICO) scoring model.

When determining if you are a good candidate, a lender will look at your credit scores. Most lenders use FICO scores, but some lenders are starting to look at Vantage Scores as well to further determine your future financial risk if they were to extend an offer of credit to you.

Both scoring models use much of the same information such as the consumer's payment history, the length and type of credit they have, the amount of their credit usage, and how many recent inquiries they have on their credit file. However, if the length of your credit history is not lengthy, then you may want to more closely monitor your Vantage Score, because a FICO Score will require a minimum of six months of credit history as well as a minimum of one reported account within the last six months.

The higher the number, the lower the risk. Consumers with higher scores are more likely to get approved for credit than those with lower scores. Additionally, they also tend to get the best interest rates when they do. And they are more likely to get discounts on insurance. What is considered a "high" score depends on what type of score is being used.

If your FICO score is 840, for example, you're just 10 points shy of the highest score possible, and your credit is "super-prime." But if you have an 840 Vantage Score, it's not as spectacular, because you're 150 points away from the highest possible score.

How to Obtain a Good Credit Score?

A good credit score is what each of us aspire to obtain. After all, a credit score is one of the most important determining factors when it comes to borrowing money – and getting a low rate when you do.

"According to consensus reports, "Only 18% of Americans have "Good" credit!"

Lenders look at very specific criteria – the six C's of credit when deciding if individuals are a good credit risk. Understanding those criteria can help keep you from making credit missteps, plus help you qualify for some of the best terms available.

1. Character

You are considered to have good credit character when you live up to your financial and credit agreements. Paying bills on time and meeting financial obligations are signs of good character.

Your credit score and your credit history are good ways for a lender to learn about your character or credit reputation and how well you pay your credit obligations.

2. Capacity

Capacity is just another term for your **debt-to-income ratio,** which measures your income versus your outgo. The lower your monthly debt obligations and the higher your income, the better your capacity.

Debt payment-income ratio = $\dfrac{\text{Minimum monthly payments}}{\text{Net Income}}$

3. Capital

A potential lender also will assess your capital. Subtract all your debts from your assets, including any property that you may own, and this is your capital. Lenders and creditors like to see that you have enough capital to handle another loan or credit account before approving you for new credit.

4. Conditions

Lenders look at conditions such as the stability of your employment, your other debts and financial obligations, and how often you've moved in the past year when considering whether to approve you for a loan. The longer you've been in a job and the less frequently you've moved the more stable your life conditions appear to potential creditors and lenders.

5. Collateral

Do you have collateral? Collateral is any property or possession that can be used as security for a payment of a debt. For example, a home or automobile serve as collateral against the loans you might take out to purchase them. Lenders like collateral because it guarantees them against a total loss if you fail to repay your loan. If that happens, your collateral may be sold or repossessed to repay your financial obligation.

6. Cash Flow

Do you have adequate cash flow to repay a new loan? How much income do you have coming in each month? Are you paid regularly, or does your income fluctuate based on seasonality or other factors? A lender or creditor wants to make sure you have enough cash flowing your way on a regular basis so that you can pay for a new credit obligation.

What is a credit report?

Your credit report is a document that contains your credit history. It is more than just a list of the credit you have had; it outlines detailed information about your credit background including:

- Identifying information like your name, address and social security number
- Types of credit you use (credit cards, mortgages, store credit, etc.)
- Open date for each loan or line of credit
- Balances and available credit on each loan and other lines of credit
- Payment history, including if you have ever missed a payment or paid late
- Collection accounts and charge-off accounts
- Recently opened credit lines or loans
- Information about hard credit inquiries (credit checks by potential lenders)
- Public records related to bankruptcy, tax liens or court judgments

Technically there are three versions of your credit report, because the three major credit-reporting agencies, Equifax, Experian and TransUnion, each have different methods for collecting and reporting your credit history.

Reading credit reports can be confusing at first glance, but there are codes on each report that will help you understand the data. The information on your report usually has 7-10 years of history. **(See next page for a sample credit report)**

You have a FICO Credit Score for each of the three credit bureaus: Equifax, Experian, and Transunion. Each of these scores is based on different information that each of the bureaus has for you, and as mentioned above, this available information may very well differ from bureau to bureau.

All the information contained in consumer credit reports is then compared to find patterns, and the resulting FICO credit score is solely determined by what is found on a person's individual credit file. This information is what will then help estimate the level of future risk there may be if a lender extends to you the offer of a loan or any other credit.

SAMPLE CREDIT REPORT

PERSONAL PROFILE

Below is your personal information as it appears in your credit file. This information includes your legal name, current and previous addresses, employment information and other details.

	Experian	Equifax	TransUnion
Name:			
Also Known As:			
Year of Birth:			
Address(es):			
Current Employer:			
Previous Employer(s):			

CREDIT SUMMARY

Below is an overview of your present and past credit status including open and closed accounts and balance information

	Experian
Real Estate Account	
Count:	
Balance:	
Current:	
Closed:	
Revolving Accounts	
Count:	
Balance:	
Current:	
Closed:	
Installment Accounts:	
Count:	
Balance:	
Current:	
Closed:	
Other Accounts	
Count:	
Balance:	
Current:	
Closed:	
Derogatory Summary:	
Inquiries:	
Public Records:	
Collections Accounts:	
Current Delinquencies:	
Prior Delinquencies:	

CREDIT INQUIRIES

Below are the names of people and/or organizations who have obtained a copy of your Credit Report. Inquiries such as these can remain on your credit file for up to two years,

BK OF AMER
Bank Credit Cards
11/7/xxxx
CHASE CARD
Banks and S&Ls
4/10/xxxx
NISSAN MOTOR
Finance other than personal
9/28/xxxx
APPLE NISSAN
Automotive
9/26/xxxx
MB FIN SVCS
Finance, personal
9/25/xxxx
APPLE CHEVRO
Automotive
9/22/xxxx
LANCASTER CN
Automotive
9/8/xxxx

PUBLIC RECORDS

Below is an overview of your public records and can include details of bankruptcy filings, court records, tax liens and other monetary judgments. Public records typically remain on your Credit Report for 7-10 years.

Experian	Equifax
There are 0 public record items on your report.	There are 0 public record items on your report.

CREDIT SCORE

Your Credit Score is a representation of your overall credit health. Most lenders utilize some form of credit scoring to help determine your credit worthiness.

XXX on Experian   XXX on Equifax   XXX on TransUnion

ACCOUNT HISTORY

Below is information on any accounts you may have opened in the past. Accounts that are paid as agreed can remain on your report for up to 10 years from the date of last activity. Typically, a consumer reporting agency will not report negative information that is more than seven years old, or bankruptcies that are more than 10 years old.

Name

	Experian	Equifax	TransUnion
Account Name:	Name	Name	Name
Account Number:	020920XXXXXX	020920XXXXXX	209207XXXXX
Account Type:	Auto Lease	Installment	Installment account
Account Status:	Closed	Closed	Closed
Monthly Payment:		$255.00	$255.00
Date Opened:	12/1/2013	12/1/2013	12/31/2013
Balanced:		$0.00	$0.00
Terms:	36 Months		36 Months
High Balance:		$9,199.00	$9,199.00
Limit:			
Past Due:			$0.00
Payment Status:	Paid satisfactorily	Pays account as agreed	Paid or paying as agreed
Comments:		PAID ACCOUNT/ZERO BALANCE AUTO	Closed

24-Month Payment History

Date:	Mar	Apr	May	Jun	Jul	Aug	Sep	Oct	Nov	Dec	Jan	Feb	Mar	Apr	May	Jun	Jul	Aug	Sep	Oct	Nov	Dec	Jan	Feb
	14	14	14	14	14	14	14	14	14	14	15	15	15	15	15	15	15	15	15	15	15	15	16	16
	OK	OK	OK	OK	OK	OK	OK	OK	OK	OK	OK	OK	OK	OK	OK	OK	OK	OK	OK	OK	OK	OK	OK	OK
	OK	OK	OK	OK	OK	OK	OK	OK	OK	OK	OK	OK	OK	OK	OK	OK	OK	OK	OK	OK	OK	OK	OK	OK
	OK	Ok	OK	Ok	OK	Ok	OK	Ok	OK	Ok	OK	Ok	OK	Ok	OK	Ok	OK	Ok	OK	Ok	OK	Ok		

Legend X

OK	Current	90	90 Days Late
ND	No Data Provided*	120	120 Days Late
30	30 Days Late	KD	Key Derogatory**
60	60 Days Late	RF	Repossession or Foreclosure
		PP	Payment Plan

*Sometimes the credit bureaus do not have information from a particular month on file.

Some lenders review your credit score; some check out your credit report and some look at both. Because of this, both are important.

Managing your Credit

Is reviewing your free annual credit report enough? **NO**
It is important to regularly check your credit report for errors and for occurrences of identity theft. This is vital because your credit score is based on what is contained in your credit report. If you wait a year to check your credit report, your credit may be damaged by the time you catch errors or fraudulent activity.

Protect yourself with affordable daily credit report monitoring

Monitoring your credit report more often can take up a lot of your time and may become overwhelming. However, you can have the peace of mind of daily credit report monitoring without the headache. **(Privacy Guard or Life Lock are a few credit monitoring companies)**

According to the National Association of State Public Interest Research Groups, 79% of all credit reports contain errors of some kind, and 20% contain serious errors. For example, I accidently washed one of my credit cards and called the creditor to have it replaced. The company reported to the bureau my card was stolen, which subsequently caused my score to drop 60 points. At the time, I had a 760-credit score, so I went from having excellent credit to good with one mistake. Imagine if I was making a purchase within that timeframe, it would have a negative effect on my interest rate.

The Federal Fair Credit Reporting Act **(FCRA)** gives you the right to dispute errors you find in your credit report. The FCRA requires that the lender provide you with the name(s) and address(s) of the credit bureau that supplied the information used in the credit screening process. After you inform the credit bureau of an error, they have 30-45 days to investigate. If the investigation confirms your claim, the credit repository must provide you with a written report of their results and change your credit report accordingly.

What If I Find a Discrepancy on My Credit Report?

When disputing any errors on your credit report, always remember to give specific details regarding why you feel the information on your credit report is incorrect and include any evidence you may have that helps to prove the mistake.

Always make copies of all the information you send with your dispute as well, so you have it for your own records **(See a sample credit report dispute form on the next page and instructions).**

You can send a letter by certified mail with a return receipt request, so you can document when the dispute was sent and when it was received. Send all your information to the credit bureau that you are asking to investigate the item on the credit report. Making copies of what you send is also a good defense in case they were to say that you never submitted enough evidence to support your claim.

Stopping identity theft before it ruins your credit

Identity theft is on the rise.
Technologically advanced criminals can use your existing lines of credit or open new credit accounts in your name. Just a little bit of personal information is all they need to steal your identity and ruin your credit.

The more fraudulent activity in your name, the more difficult it will be to restore your credit when you discover the problem.

To avoid an ID thief ruining your credit, you should check your report on a regular basis as well as adding fraud alert.

What is a Fraud Alert?

A fraud alert is a notice that is placed on your credit report that alerts credit card companies and others who may extend you credit. Think of it as a "red flag" that makes companies take steps to verify your identity before extending credit in your name.

You may contact any of the three nationwide credit bureaus – Equifax, Experian and TransUnion – to request a fraud alert. Once you place an alert with one of the bureaus, that bureau will send your request to the other two bureaus.

Fraud alerts can be placed on your credit reports for free, and there are two

Credit Report Dispute Form

If you feel there are inaccuracies in your Credit Report, you must contact each of the three major credit reporting agencies in whose report the information appears. Please complete this form and send to the addresses below (as applicable) along with two forms of ID: one copy of a government-issued identification card (such as a driver's license or a state or military ID card); and one copy of a utility bill, bank or insurance statement.

Remember, there is no charge for submitting a dispute. And for your safety, do not include original copies of the documents you use to support your dispute.

Print the name and account number of the creditor in question in the Creditor   Name/Account Number fields. Check off or clearly print the specific reason for your dispute.

Creditor Name _____ Account Number _____

Dispute Reason(s)

☐ Not My Account   ☐ Account Status Not Correct   ☐ Late Payments

☐ Paid in Full   ☐ Incorrect Balance (Approx. Correct Balance) _____

☐ Identity Theft   ☐ Other (Explain) _____

Enter Additional Information to be Corrected (For Example: Name, Address, Employer):

_____

_____

Clearly fill out all the information below, then sign the form where indicated.

First Name _____ Middle _____ Last _____

Jr. _____ Sr. _____

Address _____

City _____ State _____ Zip _____

Previous Address (if moved within the past two years) _____

City _____ State _____ Zip _____

Telephone Number _____

Social Security # (Necessary to Access Your Credit Reports) ___ ___ ___-___ ___-___ ___ ___ ___

Signature _____ Date _____

Remember to make a copy for your records.

Mail the entire form to either TransUnion, Equifax, or Experian, using the appropriate address listed below. To file online, you can enter one of the following Web addresses listed below.

Transunion: P.O. Box 2000, Chester, PA 19022
              http://annualcreditreport.transunion.com/entry/disputeonline

Equifax: P.O. Box 740256, Atlanta, GA 30374
              https://www.ai.equifax.com/CreditInvestigation/initLoginDisputePage.action

Experian: P.O. Box 4500, Allen, TX 75013
              www.experian.com/rs/fi67.html

different types:

An initial (one-year) fraud alert can be placed if you believe you are or may become a victim of fraud or identity theft. The fraud alert lasts for one year. If you want to keep it active on your credit report, you'll need to renew it after that time. When you or someone else attempts to open an account in your name or make changes on an existing account, such as increasing the credit limit, the company must take reasonable steps to confirm you are who you say you are, such as contacting you by phone at a number you provide, before completing the request. An initial fraud alert also allows you to request a free copy of your credit report each year from the three nationwide credit bureaus, in addition to the one free copy from each credit bureau you're entitled to under the Fair Credit Reporting Act.

An extended fraud alert can be placed if you are a victim of fraud or identity theft. It requires a copy of a valid police or law enforcement agency report, or a Federal Trade Commission Identity Theft Report. An extended fraud alert is like an initial fraud alert, but lasts for seven (7) years. With an extended fraud alert, a lender or creditor is required to verify your identity in person or by phone at a number you provide before opening new accounts or making changes to existing accounts.

If you have an extended fraud alert on your credit reports, you can request two free credit reports each year from the three nationwide credit bureaus.

Go to **www.equifax.com** and follow these steps to download your fraud alert form.

- Scroll down and click on "Request a fraud alert"
- Scroll down and click on "Fraud alerts & active duty alerts"
- Scroll down and click on "What is Fraud alert?
- Scroll down and click on "Alert Request form"

(Sample copy of the form is on the next page)

Once you completed the process, it will be virtually impossible for anyone to steal your identity and open accounts without your authorization.

EQUIFAX   **Alert Request Form**

To place an initial one-year fraud alert or active duty alert on your Equifax credit report, please send - via U.S. Mail- a photocopy of one item from each of the categories below to verify your identity and address. The item you select from the "Identity" category must contain your Social Security number and the item you select from the "address" category must contain your current mailing address.

Identity   Address

*Social Security card   * Driver's license or state identification card
*Pay stub with Social Security number   * Rental lease agreement/house deed
*W2 or 1099 form   * Pay stub with address
                                            * Utility bill (gas, electric, water, cable,
                                              residential telephone bill)

Alert Type: ☐ Initial One-Year Fraud Alert   ☐ Active Duty Alert

_____   _____   _____ _____
First Name   Last Name   Initial   Suffix

_____   _____   _____ _____
Current Address   City   State   Zip Code

_____   _____   _____ _____
Former Address   City   State   Zip Code

_____   _____   _____
Daytime Telephone Number   Evening Telephone Number   Cell Phone Number

_____   _____
Social Security Number   Date of Birth

Placing an initial one-year fraud alert or active duty alert is free.

Please send (via U.S. mail) this form along with the requested information to:

Equifax Information Services LLC
P.O. Box 105069
Atlanta, GA 30348-5069

Equifax Information Services LLC

Establishing a credit history

Even without a past use of credit, you may have already started building your credit history. When you are trying to establish credit, you may need to find methods to do this without qualifying for standard credit cards.

You can establish a credit history by:

- Opening bank accounts (Credit Unions preferably)
- Apartment and/or utilities in your name
- Work history (Remaining in the same job for an extended period-of-time)
- Residence history (Remaining in the same address for an extended period-of-time)
- Gas & store cards (Typically higher interest charges, but easier to obtain)
- Secured credit cards or charge cards (credit cards with no revolving credit - balance must be paid in full each month)
- Car or student loans

What is a bad credit score? (650 and below)

Your credit score is used by lenders to determine if you are a good candidate to extend credit to. However, a low credit score can flag you as a credit risk and may make it difficult to get credit.

If you are offered credit with a bad credit score, you will most likely pay more in fees and charges because you may qualify only for a higher interest rate.

Bad credit doesn't have to follow you forever

Job loss, a bad economy or simply the mismanagement of credit can put you in a situation where you have bad credit. However, bad credit does not have to follow you around for the rest of your life.

Most negative notations on your credit report will cease appearing in your credit history after seven (7) years (although some may take longer). With hard work and determination, you can watch your credit score rise.

Credit

Here are 10 Credit Tips:

1. Never use a credit card if you don't have the cash for the same amount you are borrowing in the bank. Remember, credit cards are a 25-day interest free loan!

2. Be smart, use credit cards as a budgeting tool for tracking spending.

3. Unless you are building your credit score, never apply for or utilize department store, gas or lending institution with high interest rate credit cards.

4. Focus on obtaining big six bank credit cards, which include Bank of America, Chase, Capital One, U.S Bank, Wells Fargo, and Citigroup. There are a few others, but these are the main ones that offer good rates, the best cash back incentives, and are most recognizable by credit agencies.

5. Always work with the original creditor to pay off past due payments. You want to avoid paying collections agencies!

6. Always pay credit card payments and revolving loans first and by or before the due date.

7. Set up as many automatic payments as possible.

8. Always shop for lower interest rates.

9. Only open accounts when it makes financial sense.

10. If your financial situations change and you start falling behind on your monthly payments, always call the creditor and explain your situation and plan repayment options. The worst thing you can do is not communicate and ignore the creditor.

Credit

Conclusion:

Good credit does matter!

I did a financial seminar in Harrisburg, PA a few years ago and afterwards a couple stated, "Good information Micah, but credit is overrated." I asked them why did they feel that way? They told me despite having bad credit they were able to purchase a fully loaded mini-van. I asked them if I could see their contract of purchase. Kind of personal right! I agree, but I wanted to show them visually the difference between good credit and bad. They purchased a used mini-van for $17,000 dollars that had a present value of $13,000 dollars. To make matters worse, they financed the van for 60 months at a 17% interest rate. The average APR for a used car financed 49-60 months with good credit was 4% at the time. In summary, by the end of the loan they would have paid $25,000 dollars for a vehicle that had a present value of only $13,000 dollars. This was because of their credit worthiness. If they would have understood the value of good credit, they could have purchased a newer vehicle from a reputable dealership with a greater present value and a lower interest rate.

As I stated in the beginning of the chapter, good credit gives you purchasing power. That means you will pay less interest over time when you borrow money. For example, the most important investment many Americans will make in their lifetime is buying a home. If you're purchasing a $200,000-dollar house with a 30-year fixed mortgage, and you have good credit, you could end up paying more than $130,000 dollars less for that house over the life of the loan versus if you had bad credit. So, in the end, it really pays to understand your credit scores and to make them as strong as possible.

To build and maintain a good credit score, you'll need to make all your loan payments on time, keep the amount of debt you owe below at least 30% and ideally 10% of your total credit limit(s), maintain credit accounts for the long haul, add a mix of accounts (installment loans versus revolving loans), and manage how often you apply for new credit in a short timeframe.

I realized years ago by establishing good credit increased my financial options and investment opportunities. Today, you can start your path to recapture financial freedom for yourself. When I started my journey in the summer of 2003, I was in financial despair, but I was able to persevere through due diligence and commitment to managing my finances and not allowing my finances to manage me. By 2006, I learned how to use credit properly which enabled me to avoid paying any interest on my debt. No matter what your credit rating is today, you can improve it by applying the principles and tips outlined in this chapter.

Notes:

Key Points:

_____

_____

_____

_____

_____

_____

_____

_____

How can I apply this in my life?

_____

_____

_____

_____

Action plan or next steps:

_____

_____

_____

_____

CHAPTER 5
Investing

"Investing is laying out money now to
get more money back in the future."
Warren Buffett

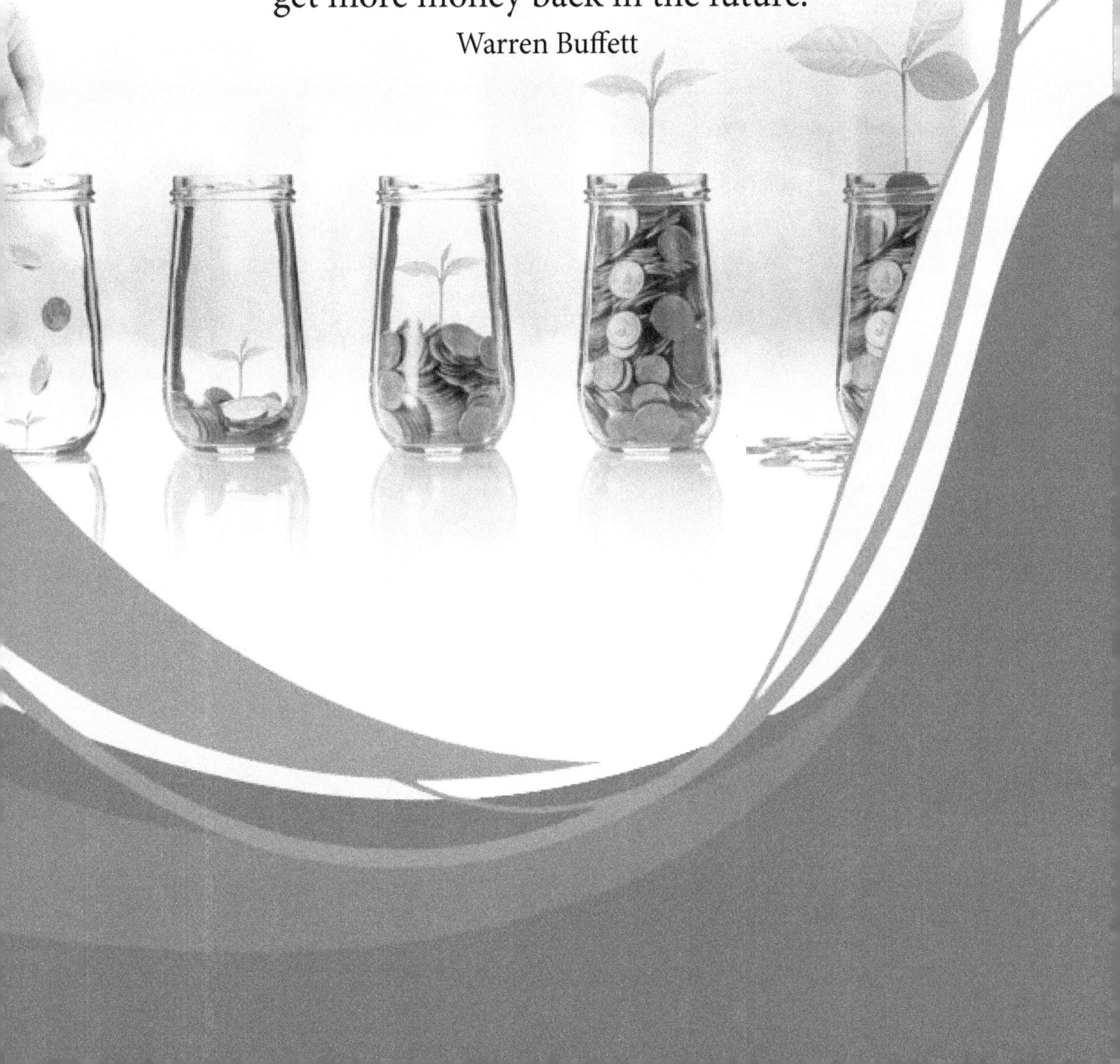

Investing

In the introduction of the workbook, I talked about creating Passive Income. Passive income is earnings derived from a rental property, limited partnership or other enterprises in which a person is not actively involved.

You are investing in various business ventures and the return nets you income. Ultimately this should be your long-term goal after you have applied all the principles from the previous chapters. Investing requires patience, so you can't be dependent upon quick returns. In addition, when making certain investments like real estate, you should utilize capital from lending institutions rather than your own cash. Therefore, establishing a good credit score is very important, because it gives you purchasing power to obtain lines of credit at low interest rates.

There are many types of investments and investing styles to choose from. Mutual funds, ETFs, individual stocks and bonds, closed-end mutual funds, real estate, various alternative investments and owning all or part of a business are just a few examples.

Stocks

Buying shares of stock gives the buyer the opportunity to participate in the company's success via increases in the stock's price and dividends that the company might declare. Shareholders have a claim on the company's assets in the event of liquidation, but do not own the assets.

Holders of common stock have voting rights at shareholders' meetings and the right to receive dividends if they are declared. Holders of preferred stock don't have voting rights but do receive preference in terms of the payment of any dividends over common shareholders. They also have a higher claim on company assets than holders of common stock.

Bonds

Bonds are debt instruments whereby an investor effectively is loaning money to a company or agency (the issuer) in exchange for periodic interest payments plus the return of the bond's face amount when the bond matures. Bonds are issued by corporations, the federal government plus many states, municipalities and governmental agencies.

A typical corporate bond might have a face value of $1,000 and pay interest semi-annually. Interest on these bonds are fully taxable, but interest on municipal bonds is exempt from federal taxes and may be exempt from state taxes for residents of the issuing state. Interest on Treasuries are taxed at the federal level only.

Bonds can be purchased as new offerings or on the secondary market, just like stocks. A bond's value can rise and fall based on several factors, the most important being the direction of interest rates. Bond prices move inversely with the direction of interest rates.

Mutual funds

A mutual fund is a pooled investment vehicle managed by an investment manager that allows investors to have their money invested in stocks, bonds or other investment vehicles as stated in the fund's prospectus.

Mutual funds are valued at the end of trading day and any transactions to buy or sell shares are executed after the market close as well.

Mutual funds can passively track stock or bond market indexes such as the S&P 500, the Barclay's Aggregate Bond Index and many others. Other mutual funds are actively managed where the manager actively selects the stocks, bonds or other investments held by the fund. Actively managed mutual funds are generally costlier to own. A fund's underlying expenses serve to reduce the net investment returns to the mutual fund shareholders.

Mutual funds can make distributions in the form of dividends, interest and capital gains. These distributions will be taxable if held in a non-retirement account. Selling a mutual fund can result in a gain or loss on the investment, just as with individual stocks or bonds.

Mutual funds allow small investors to instantly buy diversified exposure to several investment holdings within the fund's investment objective. For instance, a foreign stock mutual might hold 50 or 100 or more different foreign stocks in the portfolio. An initial investment as low as $1,000 (or less in some cases) might allow an investor to own all the underlying holdings of the fund. Mutual funds are a great way for investors large and small to achieve a level of instant diversification.

ETFs

ETFs or exchange-traded funds are like mutual funds in many respects but are traded on the stock exchange during the trading day just like shares of stock. Unlike mutual funds which are valued at the end of each trading day, ETFs are valued constantly while the markets are open.

Many ETFs track passive market indexes like the S&P 500, the Barclay's Aggregate Bond Index, and the Russell 2000 index of small cap stocks and many others.
In recent years, actively managed ETFs have come into being, as have so-called smart beta ETFs which create indexes based on "factors" such as quality, low volatility and momentum.

Alternative Investments

Beyond stocks, bonds, mutual funds and ETFs, there are many other ways to invest. Real estate investments can be made by buying a commercial or residential property directly.

"90% of all millionaires become so through owning real estate" (Andrew Carnegie). Real estate is a huge industry and there are a lot of opportunities to invest in real estate. But where should you start? What types of real estate investing is best for you? Learning the basics of how to invest in real estate is the first step in choosing a strategy. You can then explore different real estate investment strategies and pick one based on your time, budget, and long-term goals.

There are 6 different real estate investment strategies:

1) Buy and Holds

These are good, long-term investments because of the steady additional income and the opportunity to gain appreciation. If looking for an active, long-term investment, buy-and-holds are the way to go.

Buying an investment property as a buy-and-hold requires research about the market, neighborhood, and property expenses. Positive cash flow is very important with these investment because money is otherwise lost every month. With buy-and-holds, deciding on becoming a landlord or hiring property management is also something to consider. Can you manage the property yourself? Can you handle having tenants?

Not all buy-and-hold properties are the same. These can range from single-family homes to entire apartment buildings. Depending on location and cash flow, an investor might choose to rent out an entire single-family home to a family or rent out individual rooms to individual tenants. Multi-family homes are popular if the investor wants to have a personal residence at the same location as their investments. The advantage with multi-family homes is being able to spend less and gain more. Finally, apartment buildings can range from small to large buildings. When owning an apartment building, you are becoming the home owner association (HOA), and can create your own rules to follow.

2) Airbnb Investment Properties

These are also a type of buy-and-hold property, but are vacation or short-term rentals. When buying an investment property as a vacation rental, there are different things to consider. Can you manage turnover between tenants? What are the occupancy rates like in your area? What are the legal regulations for having a short-term rental or Airbnb investment property?

There has been an increase in the number of Airbnb investors as Airbnb investment properties have proved to be lucrative and sometimes produce more income than traditional investments.

3) Fix and Flips

Fix-and-flips are for investors looking for active, short-term investments to quickly make money. Fix-and-flips are properties that are bought, renovated and then sold. They are not a get-rich quick scheme but if done correctly, investors can quickly profit from this strategy.

When looking for a property to flip, it's important to look for deal-breakers. After setting a budget, it's crucial to consult an inspector, contractor and appraiser in order to identify issues and avoid losing time and money. When flipping, time is the biggest asset. The longer it takes to flip the property, the more monthly expenses.

4) Commercial

The U.S. commercial market is huge and joining commercial real estate investing can lead to huge returns. These properties are leased to businesses which can range from tiny little stores to shopping malls. While there's an opportunity to rent out to big businesses and get significant cash flow, vacancies can last longer than with residential properties. This strategy is not for beginners, but it's a great level to reach in your real estate portfolio. Read more in the next point about how you can do this.

5) Passive Investments

Passively investing in real estate means not getting your hands dirty and giving your money to someone else to make the investment happen. One way to do this is by working with a Real Estate Investment Trust (REIT), which is when a group of investors pool their money to buy large real estate investments, such as malls, skyscrapers, or many single-family homes. Each investor gets a share of the profits and does very little work. These passive investments generally have higher returns and less risk. Different types of REITs include retail, residential, healthcare, office and mortgage REITs. An investor can invest in a stock exchange-listed REIT or buy a share in a REIT mutual fund. It's best to consult a financial expert to see if this real estate investment strategy would be for you.

Another way to passively invest in real estate is lending your money to an investor looking for a property to flip. Why wouldn't an investor just go to a bank? It's difficult to get a loan for a property that is vacant and needs work. This loan is called a "First Trust Deed" investment. The investors should pay the 20% down payment and closing costs. As a lender, you would receive interest payments on the loan and a final payment at the end of the term. Your money is secured by the property.

6) Real Estate Wholesaling

Making money in real estate does not always require spending money, there are so many diverse opportunities to invest. Wholesaling is one of the ways you can create income without having to spend any money at all. A wholesaler finds a seller who wants to put their property up for sale and has not yet gone on the market. The wholesaler finds a buyer and then is entitled to a share of the selling price. To be successful with the real estate investment strategy, you must network and make contacts in order to have a database of potential sellers and buyers.

Hedge funds and private equity also fall into the category of alternative investments, although they are only open to those who meet the income and net worth requirements of being an accredited investor. Hedge funds may invest almost anywhere and may hold up better than conventional investment vehicles in turbulent markets.

Conclusion

As you can see, there are many ways to increase your income by investing savings and spending money wisely. This can be a fun and rewarding process, but it can also be complicated and risky. Not all types of investments are guaranteed to make you money and sometimes you can lose the money you already have.

If you have started to set aside money, you may want to find a financial advisor to help you make financial decisions. This may be a trusted friend or relative who handles their own money successfully, someone at a bank or financial institution whom you trust, or a lawyer or stockbroker at a reliable company.

Whomever you choose, be sure they have a good reputation, are trustworthy, make you feel comfortable, can clearly show how they are handling your money and what they are charging you for. Above all, be sure that you keep control over your money! Your advisor may make suggestions about how to handle your money, but you should know what is happening to your money and make all final decisions.

Notes:

Key Points:

_____

_____

_____

_____

_____

_____

_____

_____

How can I apply this in my life?

_____

_____

_____

_____

_____

Action plan or next steps:

_____

_____

_____

_____

_____

CHAPTER 6
Conclusion and Acknowledgements

Manage Your Money Before It Manages You

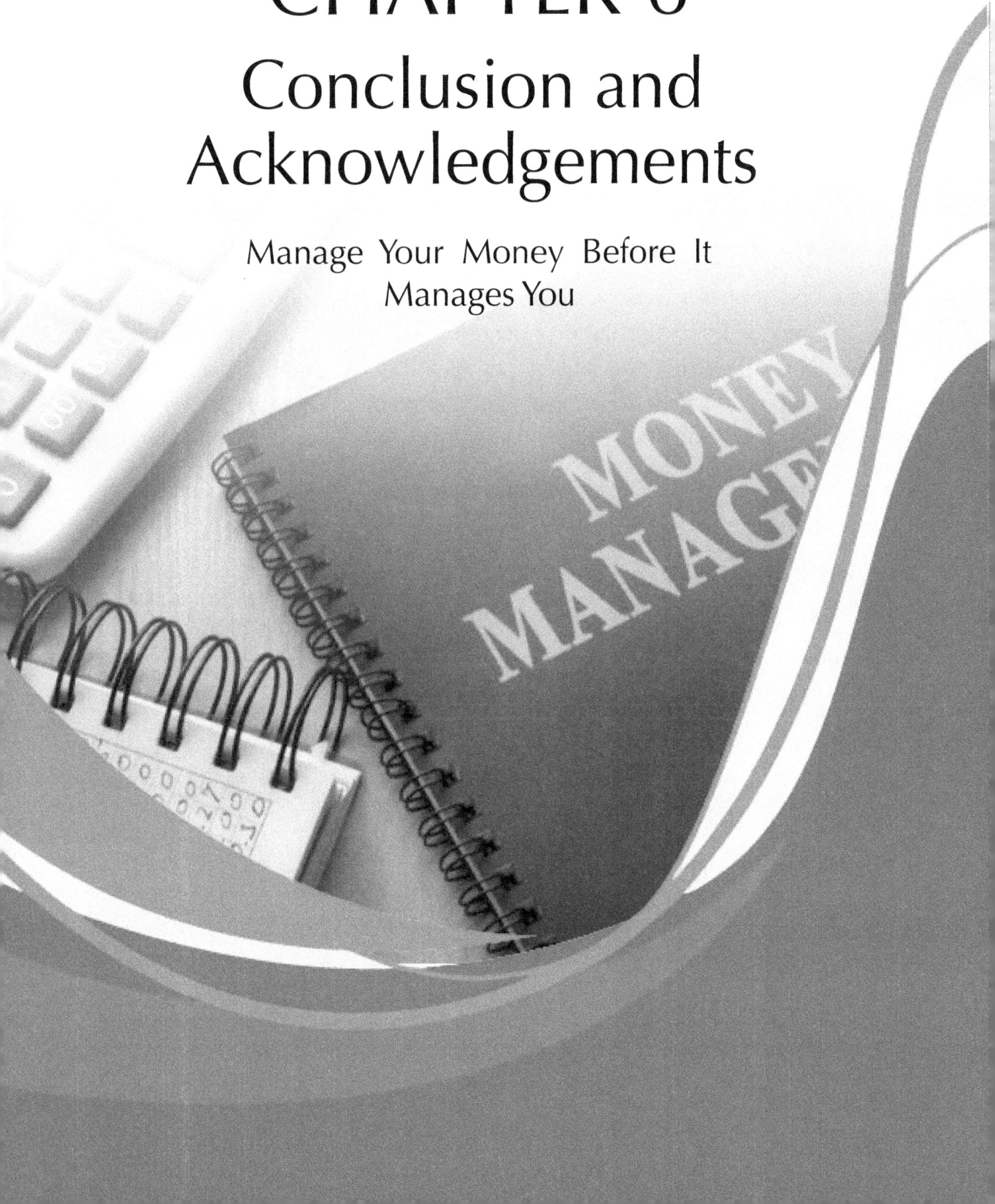

Conclusion

Today, I'm debt free, with a near perfect credit score, along with several profitable investments. My path to financial security wasn't always easy, but I persevered through the tough times. It started with my renewed mindset regarding finances, which dictated a change in my spending habits. As a result, I began to behave responsibly when it came to my approach about money. I've always been adamant that how you think about money is an important, if not the most important, part of personal finance.

Your money mindset is the feelings and thoughts you subconsciously develop towards money from your life experiences. Because our thoughts often control our actions, developing a negative money mindset can create a barrier between you and financial health. It can keep you in a place of stress and anxiety, which will keep you from achieving financial goals.

If you've developed a negative mindset around money, it doesn't mean this is how you'll always feel.

You can shift your bad money thoughts to a positive, more productive mindset by applying the following steps:

Recognize self-sabotaging thoughts

Step one always seems to be the hardest, and this is no exception. Being aware enough to recognize any sabotaging thoughts is not easy, but without doing this you won't be able to improve your mindset. Some examples of common self-sabotaging, negative thoughts are:

- I'll never get out of debt
- I don't make enough to save
- I'll never be able to afford that
- I'll never make as much as so-and-so

Take time to reflect on things you've thought or said in the past. If nothing comes to mind, make a conscious effort to keep track of how you feel or what you say when the topic of money comes up. What happens when an unexpected bill comes in or when you don't receive a raise that you were expecting? Make a note of it, even if it feels like the truth and not a self-sabotaging thought and reflect on how that thought is affecting your actions.

Appreciate what you have

If you concentrate on what you don't have, you will never, ever have enough. Being appreciative for what you have is the best way to start to shake your negative thoughts or self-sabotaging behaviors. We all have so much to be thankful for and while we may sometimes recognize this, when it comes to money and budgeting many of us tend to take a restrictive view that can bring us down.

In the beginning of my financial journey, I struggled with negative thoughts towards my credit card debt. I used to only look at my balances as a burden—a huge debt that was keeping me from other financial goals in my life. Once I realized this negative thought pattern, I tried to focus on what that represented and what I have. I am thankful that I had the opportunity to travel, pay for my educational goals, and more importantly, that I had a job that enabled me to pay off my commitments. By letting go of the negativity of the debt and focusing on what it brought me eased the mental burden and stress about it less.

Forgive yourself for past mistakes

We tend to be our own worst critic and for many people, making a financial mistake is something that we hold onto forever. But holding on to that negativity and beating yourself up for mistakes you've made in the past can keep you from moving forward. Maybe you've made some bad choices, spent too much money, or landed yourself in a heap of debt. Give yourself the permission to forgive yourself and look at these mistakes as learning opportunities. Know that no one is perfect and remember that what matters most is how you move forward from that mistake. I made a financial decision in 2005 that wiped out most of my savings, but I learned not to be anxious when executing business transactions. I was very frustrated with myself at the time, but I chose to move on from the situation and use the incident as a learning opportunity. Forgiving yourself, without forgetting the mistake, can help you appreciate and really learn from past experiences.

Define what you really want

It's a simple strategy, but most people don't take the time to really reflect on their wants/desires and create a plan to get there.

After completing chapter 3 of the workbook, you should have taken the time to really reflect on what you specifically desire, what you will do to reach that desire, and when you will reach it by.

Stay educated and implement your new knowledge

Being educated on money matters can help you feel confident and in control of your own future. Knowledge is wisdom gained by experience and it also gives you power. I sincerely hope this information resonates with you, because it's my goal in life to help change as many people's financial landscape as I can.

In the introduction of the workbook, there were seven (7) specific questions that I asked you to answer, so I will end by asking, "Did you pull your credit report, create a legalized will, purchase adequate life insurance, and established a budget?" All your answers should be yes. Therefore, you are on the way to obtaining an excellent credit score and establishing a strong savings account, which will lead to profitable investment opportunities in the future.

In conclusion, prosperity is the condition of being successful or thriving; economic well-being. There are different levels of prosperity, so don't define your financial success based upon another's achievements. Align your actions to meet your individual desires, and most importantly, enjoy the process and be patient with the results.

Workbook Checklist:

	Yes	No	Date Completed
1. Did you create a legalized Will?			
2. Did you get a Life Insurance policy that covers your family's needs?			
3. Did you pull your credit report?			
4. Did you complete your net-worth calculation worksheet?			
5. Did you create your account worksheet?			
6. Did you create a written budget?			
7. Did you complete your setting financial goals worksheet?			
8. Did you complete your personal goals worksheet?			
9. Did you add fraud alert to your credit report to avoid identity theft?			

Acknowledgments

I would like to start by thanking all the individuals that have approached me with their questions and shared their stories over the years, because it enabled me to learn from them. Money management is one of the hardest subjects to be fully transparent about with others. Each question you asked, every suggestion I have offered, and all the feedback that I have received, have contributed to the creation of this workbook.

I would like to thank those who have been supportive of my goal to write this workbook. I especially like to thank my spiritual father and mother, Thaddeus and Eloise Godwin, as well as my brother, pastor and best friend, Melvin Dickens. I cannot put a value on your insight and encouragement that you have given me. Nobody has been more important to me in the pursuit of this project than the members of my immediate and extended family. I would like to thank my mom, Deborah Holland, whose love and guidance are with me in whatever I pursue. I wish to thank my loving and supportive wife, Kae, and my two children, Peri and Isaiah, for their inspiration.

Finally, I give all the glory and honor to God for His strength and guidance to write this workbook. Without His presence in my life, this endeavor would not have been possible.

Sources:

1. Privacy Guard Credit Monitoring Service
    www.privacyguard.com

2. "Laying the Foundation for Success" by Carleton H. Sheets

3. LawDepot.com

4. "All Your Worth: The ultimate Lifetime Money Plan" by Senator Elizabeth Warren

5. www.equifax.com

6. Various on-line financial articles (unknown authors)

www.ingramcontent.com/pod-product-compliance
Lightning Source LLC
Chambersburg PA
CBHW081746200326
41597CB00024B/4414